William Jay Smith

COLLECTED TRANSLATIONS

COLLECTED TRANSLATIONS

Italian · French
Spanish · Portuguese

William Jay Smith

Woodcuts by Jacques Hnizdovsky

A New Rivers Abroad Book
NEW RIVERS PRESS
1985

Most of these translations have been published elsewhere. Our
thanks to the editors of these publications for permission to
reprint here. Specific acknowledgements appear on page 150 of
this volume.

Collected Translations has been published with the aid of grants
from the McKnight Foundation, the Arts Development Fund of
the United Arts Council, and the First Bank System Foundation.

Woodcut on cover: "Dahlia," 1972 by Jacques Hnizdovsky; other
woodcuts by Jacques Hnizdovsky: facing title page, "Three
Dahlias," 1970; "Onion," p. 13, 1970; "Circle of Growth," p. 25,
1967; "Rosa," p. 119, 1972; "Thistle," p. 133, 1964.

New Rivers Press books are distributed by

Bookslinger	and	Small Press Distribution
213 E. 4th St.		1784 Shattuck Ave.
St. Paul, MN		Berkeley, CA
55104		94709

Collected Translations has been manufactured in the United
States of America for New Rivers Press (C. W. Truesdale, edi-
tor/publisher), 1602 Selby Ave., St. Paul, MN 55104 in a first
edition of 1,500 copies.

To Richard Wilbur

CONTENTS

Italian

French

Spanish

Portuguese

INTRODUCTION

I have gathered together in this volume translations that I have done over the past several decades of poems in the Romance languages — Italian, French, Spanish, and Portuguese. In assembling work covering so long a period (one or two of the translations date from my undergraduate years in the nineteen thirties), I have sought to determine what principle, if any, governed my choice of the poetry translated. These are all poems that have delighted me in one way or another, and, as that inspired and omniverous reader Borges has said, without enchantment, all else is useless. They are also poems that I should have been happy to have written myself. Of a great number of the poets represented, few satisfactory translations of their work existed when I produced mine. When my volumes of the poetry of Jules Laforgue and Valery Larbaud appeared in the fifties, only a handful of poems of Laforgue (other than T. S. Eliot's reworkings) had appeared in English and almost nothing of Valery Larbaud. The latter indeed was so little known that one much-published critic made what is surely one of the most horrific blunders of the century in announcing calmly that "Valery Larbaud" was a pseudonym of Paul Valéry.

My selection includes offerings of both gold and silver, both major and minor poetry. Laforgue, whose poems concerning outer space and the destruction of the earth seem so far in advance of their time, insisted that whatever else it is, poetry must be interesting. And I hope that my choices, although they make no effort to cover any one period systematically, will prove both interesting and varied. Several of the translations are here because I was asked, sometimes by the poet himself, to undertake them. But over the years I have turned down a number of such requests when I felt no affinity for the poetry in question.

A word about my impetus to translate. Born in Louisiana and brought up just below the confluence of the Missouri and Mississippi Rivers, I became aware early on of a multi-lingual background. It seemed both necessary and desirable to be able to move from one language to another. And since the most concentrated expression in any language is in its poetry, I found it natural to attempt, whatever the difficulty, to convert that concentrated form by a similar distillation into another language. I began as a student of French and moved from a study of Old French (a Master's thesis on *Ami et Amile*, an epic fragment of the thirteenth century) to Vulgar Latin and on to Italian, Spanish, and ultimately Portuguese. In the thirties I discovered with great excitement *The Spirit of Romance* by Ezra Pound, and that book proved at the time to be the perfect guidebook to the poetry of the Mediterranean.

11

The translation of the rondeau by Voiture, with which my French section begins, possesses, for all its utterly frivolous nature, two qualities that I trust the other selections will in some way bear out — a predilection for form and a keen edge of wit. "The work of translation," Valéry wrote, "done with regard for a certain approximation of form, causes us in some way to try walking in the tracks left by the author; and not to fashion one text upon the other, but from the latter to work back to the virtual time of its formation, to the phase when the mind is in the same state as an orchestra whose instruments begin to waken, calling to each other and seeking harmony before beginning their concert. From this imagined living state one must make one's way down toward its resolution in a work in a different tongue." No better description exists of the process of poetic translation. It is the "regard for a certain approximation of form" which a good many contemporary translators, by turning everything into the freest of free verse, completely disregard.

Poetic form in one language, because it is unique, can only be approximated in another; it cannot be duplicated. Rhyme in all the Romance languages is very much easier than in English; and although I have tried in some instances to retain a rhyme scheme in its entirety, in others I have felt that to do so would destroy other qualities that the poem possesses. There are no hard-and-fast rules, and the way back into footsteps of the original poet must vary with the individual poem.

Translating poetry, I have said elsewhere, is like converging on a flame with a series of mirrors, mirrors of technique and understanding, until the flame is reflected in upon itself in a wholly new and foreign element. I hope that my manipulation of the mirrors in this selection of poems, which range from thirteenth-century Italy to present-day Brazil, has been skillful enough to keep the original flame alive and sparkling in its English reflection.

—W. J. S.

12

ITALIAN

ANONYMOUS
(XIIIth Century)

OUT FROM ITS FINE CAGE

Out from its fine cage flies the nightingale.
The little boy cries when he finds no more
His little bird in its bright new cage;
And in tears he says: "Who opened its door?"
And in tears he says: "Who opened its door?"
Then out in a wood he goes walking
And hears the sweet song of that fledgling.
"Come back to my garden, oh, sweet nightingale!
Come back to my garden, oh, sweet nightingale!"

MICHELANGELO BUONARROTI
(1475-1564)

"NIGHT" IN THE MEDICI CHAPEL

Sleep's very dear to me, but being stone's
Far more, so long as evil persevere.
It's my good fortune not to see nor hear:
Do not wake me; speak in the softest tones.

UGO FOSCOLO
(1778-1827)

SELF-PORTRAIT

My forehead's lined, my eyes intense, deep-set;
My hair full-blown, cheeks gaunt, a proud aspect;
Full curving lips, slow to give way to wit;
Fine neck with head inclined to hairy chest;
Compact in build, elegant but simply dressed;
Quick in step, in thought, in act and word;
Prodigal but sober, bristling but sincere —
When it's hostile to me, I'm hostile to the world.

Sad most days and alone; always contemplative,
Believing not in hope, not fearing fear,
Modesty makes me craven; anger, brave;
Reason counsels, but the heart will never hear,
Both vile and virtuous must wildly rave —
Death, you alone can give me fame and rest.

GIACOMO LEOPARDI
(1798-1837)

THE INFINITE

I've always liked this lonely hill
crowned with a thicket cutting from view
so great a part of the far horizon.
Sitting and gazing out, I can imagine
interminable spaces beyond, supernatural
silences, and that profound calm
in which the heart comes near
to terror. And as I hear
the wind flutter the branches around me,
I weigh its voice against that infinite
silence; and summon up Eternity,
the dead seasons, and the present one
alive with sound. And so in this Immensity
my thoughts drown; and I find how sweet
it is to shipwreck in that sea.

GIOSUÈ CARDUCCI
(1835-1907)

LEAVE-TAKING

Tri-colored flower:
stars go down far out at sea
and in my heart songs die.

GIOVANNI PASCOLI
(1855-1912)

NOVEMBER

The air gemlike, the sun so clear
that you seek apricots in flower
and find in your heart only the white
        thorn's bitter scent.

The thornbush is dry; stick-like the plants
stand now revealed in somber silhouette
against a vacant sky; and earth resounds
        with hollow step.

Silence: but hear in the distant wind
descending faintly on orchard and flowerbed
the crackling leaves — in this, the cold
        summer of the dead.

UMBERTO SABA
(1883-1957)

KITCHEN RANGE

What immense gratitude one feels toward life
for having saved these dear things,
what an ocean of delights, my soul!

Everything is so in place!
Everything still so in place!
In great poverty there is also salvation.
The beauty of the yellow polenta
moves my eye; my heart, through
the most occult charms, attains the possible
extremity of human feeling.
If I could, I would die here
where instinct drew me. Beside me
two masons dine in stony silence
and an old man who has consumed
a meal without wine
has shut himself in on himself
in the welcome heat like an unborn child
in its mother's womb. He looks a bit
like my poor wandering father
as he cursed my mother while a terrified
child listened. I feel close
to my origins: I feel,
if not mistaken, that I've returned to my own place;

to the people in whom I die, to where I was born.

GIUSEPPE UNGARETTI
(1888-1970)

MORNING

On the edge of night
I fill with the light
Of immensity.

EUGENIO MONTALE
(1896-1981)

THE EEL

The eel, that North Sea
siren who leaves the cold Baltic
for our warm seas,
our estuaries, our rivers,
swimming upstream against their currents,
climbing from branch to branch,
from stem to thinner stem,
penetrating ever deeper the core
of stone, threading
narrowing channels of ooze until one day
a flare from flowering chestnuts
kindles its flickering thread in those stagnant pools,
those hollows sweeping down
from the terraced Appenines to the Romagna,
the eel, that torch, that whip,
that arrow of Earthly Love,
which only our gullies and fiery, dried
creek beds can lead back
to paradises of fertility;
green soul that looks for life
where only drought and desolation gnaw,
spark proclaiming
that everything begins only
when it is burned out, rotted away like a stump;
brief rainbow, iris, twin
of that one you set between your lashes
and let shine in the midst of the sons
of man, sunk as they are in your primeval mud —
can you believe she is not your sister?

SALVATORE QUASIMODO
(1901-1968)

AND THEN SUDDENLY IT'S DARK

Alone at the earth's core stands each man,
Pierced by a ray of light; and then
suddenly it's dark.

FRENCH

VINCENT VOITURE
(1597-1648)

RONDEAU

Lord, I'm done for: now Margot
Insists I write her a rondeau.
Just to think of it gives me pain:
Eight "o" lines and five in "ain" —
A slow boat to China is not so slow.

With five lines down, and eight to go,
I summon Sono Osato,
Adding, with an eye for gain,
                    Lord, I'm done.

If from my brain five others flow
My poem will in beauty grow:
Comes eleven, that is plain,
And twelve to follow in its train,
And so thirteen rounds out the show —
                    Lord, I'm done!

THÉOPHILE GAUTIER
(1811-1872)

THE CHIMERA

A young Chimera at an orgy left
On my cup's rim the sweetest of all kisses;
Her eyes were green, and to her hips down-swept
The fullscale gold-red torrent of her tresses.

Her wings were the wings of a hawk; and as they rose
And fluttered to depart, I sprang upon her back.
Into her mane my hand sank like a comb,
Bringing to me her huge and willowy neck.

She howled in fury; raged, but all in vain.
In her great body deeper dug my knees
Until, in a voice as soft as silver rain,
She asked me then: "Where to, Master, please?"

"On beyond the sun, the realm of space,
Where, but for Eternity, God would be;
Your wing may tire before we reach that place;
For I must see my dream in its reality."

ARTHUR RIMBAUD
(1854-1891)

THE STROLLING PLAYER

My hands in pockets worn out at the seams,
And clad in a coat that was almost perfect, too,
I traveled, Muse, and I was true to you;
How splendid were the loves I found in dreams!

I had a large hole in my pants, my only pair.
Like Tom Thumb, dreamer lad, I formed my rhymes;
I stayed at the Sign of the Dipper several times.
My stars made a sound like silk in the high, night air.

I'd hear them on the highway when I stopped
Those good September evenings while dew dropped,
Cooling my head like wine poured in the dark;

When rhyming in those shadowed, eerie places,
Like lyre strings I'd pluck the elastic laces
Of my battered shoes, one foot against my heart.

ARTHUR RIMBAUD

THE SLEEPER IN THE VALLEY

This is the green wherein a river chants
Whose waters on the grasses wildly toss
Its silver tatters, where proud sunlight slants
Within a valley thick with beams like moss.

A youthful soldier, mouth agape, head bare,
And nape where fresh blue water cresses drain
Sleeps stretched in grass, beneath the cloud, where
On abundant green the light descends like rain.

His feet on iris roots, smiling perhaps
As would some tiny sickly child, he naps.
O nature, he is cold: make warm his bed.

This quiver of perfume will not break his rest;
In sun he sleeps, his hand on quiet breast.
Upon one side there are two spots of red.

JULES LAFORGUE
(1860-1887)

APOTHEOSIS

In all directions, forever, silence swarms
With clusters of golden stars interlacing their arcs.
One would think they were gardens sanded with diamonds,
But each one twinkles in dismal isolation.

High up in that unknown corner gleaming
Sadly with its furrow of rubies,
Now a spark is delicately blinking:
A patriarch scout who guides his family.

His family: a host of heavy, blossoming globes,
And on one, the earth, a yellow point, Paris,
Where, under a swinging lamp, a poor fool sits.

A weak phenomenon in the universal order,
Knowing himself the mirror of a single day,
He thinks of all this, then composes a sonnet.

JULES LAFORGUE

FUNERAL MARCH
FOR THE DEATH OF THE EARTH

(an announcement of the death)

Lento

O solemn procession of magnificent suns,
Knot and unknot your great golden masses,
Gently, sadly, to somber music,
Conduct your sleeping sister's slow cortège.

Time has ceased. After one last rattle,
Shaken by a sob, in the black silence
Of unechoing calm, the Earth, dead forever,
Floats like an enormous and solitary wreck.
Such a dream! Is it true? Carried off by the night,
You are now but a coffin, an inert and tragic block.
Remember, however, your unparalleled epic;
And sleep, all is over, sleep eternally.

O solemn procession of magnificent suns.

And yet remember, Earth, the early ages
When you had, in the spleen of long days,
Only pantoums of wind, rumbling waves,
And the silvery rustling of foliage.
When impure being came, weak rebel,
And tore the lovely veils from holy Maia,
And the sobbing of time engulfed the stars...
But sleep, all is over, sleep eternally.

O solemn procession of magnificent suns.

Nor will you forget the dark Middle Ages,
When to the disturbing knell of *Dies Irae*
Famine prepared its powdered bones
For Pestilence, furiously gorging the charnel houses.
Remember the time when hopeless, cringing man,
Still obstinately begging for Mercy,
Cried "Glory to God," and cursed his race!
But sleep, all is over, sleep eternally.

O solemn procession of magnificent suns.

Hymns, bloody altars, somber cathedrals
With mournful windows, incense amid the bells;
And organs pouring forth their powerful hosannahs!
O white forsaken cloisters, pale claustral loves,
That hysterical century when doubting man
Found himself alone without Justice, without God,
Rolling in the unknown on an ephemeral globe.
But sleep, all is over, sleep eternally.

O solemn procession of magnificent suns.

And stakes, lead, torture, prisons,
Asylums, towers, brothels,
Old invention, music, arts
And sciences, war fattening the countryside.
And luxury, spleen, love, charity.
Hunger, thirst, alcohol, ten thousand maladies.
Oh, what a drama lies in these cool ashes.
But sleep, all is over, sleep eternally.

O solemn procession of magnificent suns.

Where then is Buddha, chaste and sublime,
Who bled for all mankind and wrote his good law,
And sad and gentle Jesus who doubted the faith
By which he lived, for which he died?
All those who have wept over the atrocious enigma?
Where are their books as meaningless as madness?
Oh, how many others unknown bled in silence.
But sleep, all is over, sleep eternally.

O solemn procession of magnificent suns.

No more the marble Venus, the frivolous etchings.
The mad brain of Hegel, sweet consoling refrains,
Steeples embroidered with sunlight, consumed with flights,
Books, the record of man's futile victories.
All that the fury of your sons has engendered,
All that was your filth and your brief splendor,
O Earth, is now a dream, a great dream.
Come, sleep, all is over, sleep eternally.

O solemn procession of magnificent suns.

Sleep eternally, it is over, you may think
Of this extraordinary drama as but a nightmare;
You are now but a tomb that drags along
Its nameless cadaver in the immemorial dark.
It was a dream, oh, yes, you have never been.
Everything is alone; nothing sees nor thinks.
There is only dark, time and silence.
Sleep, you have dreamed, sleep eternally.

O solemn procession of magnificent suns,
Knot and unknot your great golden masses,
Gently, sadly, to somber music,
Conduct your sleeping sister's slow cortège.

THE IMPOSSIBLE

Tonight I may die. Rain, wind, sun
Will scatter everywhere my heart, my nerves, my marrow.
All will be over for me. Neither sleep nor awakening.
I shall not have been out there among the stars.

In every direction, I know, on those distant worlds,
Are similar pilgrims of pale solitudes,
Extending us their hands across the gentle dark,
Sister humanities dreaming in multitudes.

Yes, brothers everywhere. That I know, I know.
And all alone like us. Trembling with sadness,
They beckon to us at night. Ah, shall we never go?
We would console one another in our great distress.

The stars, it is certain, will one day meet,
Heralding perhaps that universal dawn
Now sung by those beggars with caste marks of thought.
A fraternal outcry will be raised against God.

Alas, before that time, rain, wind, sun
Will have lost in the distance my heart, my nerves, my marrow.
All will be done without me. Neither dream nor awakening.
I shall not have been among the gentle stars.

JULES LAFORGUE

THE CIGARETTE

Indeed, this world is flat: as for the other, nonsense.
With hopeless resignation I accept my fate,
And to kill time while I await
Death, smoke thin cigarettes in the face of the gods.

Go, struggle on, poor skeletons to be.
As for me, the blue stream that winds heavenward
Plunges me in an infinite ecstasy and drugs
Me like the dying scent of a thousand perfume jars.

And I enter paradise, blossoming with clear dreams,
Where one sees, coupled in fantastic waltzes,
Choirs of mosquitoes and elephants in heat.

And when I awake thinking of my poem,
With joyous heart I contemplate
My dear thumb roasted like a drumstick.

COMPLAINT OF THE MOON
IN THE PROVINCES

Ah, the lovely full Moon,
As big as a fortune!

In the distance sounds retreat,
His Honor, the Alderman, goes by;

A clavichord plays across the street,
A cat runs across the square;

And the provinces go to sleep.
Resounding with a final chord,

The piano covers up its keys.
What time is it, what time can it be?

What exile for the peaceful Moon!
Must one say: so it shall be?

Moon, oh, dilettante Moon,
With all climates in common,

You saw the Missouri yesterday,
And now the ramparts of Paris,

The blue fjords of Norway,
The poles, the oceans, and what else?

Happy Moon! So now you see
The end of the marriage ceremony.

The bride on her wedding trip
Has left for Scotland on a ship.

What a trap if this winter she
Had taken my lines literally.

Moon, vagrant Moon,
Shall we team up, and go our way?

O wealthy nights, I depart
This life, the provinces on my heart!

And the moon, old woman, wears
Wads of cotton in her ears.

ANOTHER COMPLAINT
OF LORD PIERROT

Here's the woman who will make all womankind crystal clear!
So before she starts, let us tell her with perfect ease:
"The sum of the angles of a triangle, sweetheart dear,
    Is equal to one hundred and eighty degrees."

She: "God, but I love you, my darling, you are a dream!"
I: "God will reward his own, I do believe."
She, cut to the quick: "You're my keyboard's only theme."
    I: "All is purely relative."

Then, opening wide her eyes, quite run-of-the mill,
She says: "If you don't love me, there are plenty of others who do!"
One eye intent upon the Unconscious still,
    I answer: "Thank you, not bad; and you?"

"Let's play at Faithfulness!" "What on earth is the use?"
"One might as well play to lose, that much is clear."
"And you'll be the first to tire of it, I am sure."
    "After you, if it please you, dear."

And when upon my page one night she dies — how
Lovely! — I, feigning not to believe she is dead,
Will murmur: "With so much to live for, really now!
    Did we mean everything we said?"

COMPLAINT OF
THE KING OF THULE

Once there was a King of Thule,
    An immaculate King was he,
Who far from petticoats and the like
Mourned the metempsychosis
    By which lilies became roses,
    What a palace was his!

On milky nights, past his sleeping flowers,
    He would go, dragging his keys,
To embroider on a high tower
A certain bright-colored sail,
    The stars his only witnesses.

When he had finished hemming the sail,
He departed on the gray seas,
    Far from Thule,
Rowing hard toward the dying sun,
That failing temple of delight,
    And so would wail:

"Dying sun, for one day more
Your beacon light has beckoned forth
All the viviparous holocausts
Of the cult which men call love.

"And now as you feel your strength fail
Before the wild night falls,
You come to bathe the alcove
With one last wave of martyred blood.

"Sun! Sun! See me descending
Now toward your heart-rending
Polar palaces to rock to sleep
        Your bleeding heart
        In this Winding Sheet."

He spoke, and with the sail full-spread,
        Agitated and dismayed,
As handsome as one of the Wise Men,
The King, mocked by petticoats,
        Descended then
        To wrecked ships and coral reefs.

Gentle lovers, on milky nights,
        Do not fail to turn the key!
A phantom chilled with pure love
Might come to sing you this old saw:
"Once there was a King of Thule,
        An immaculate King was he..."

COMPLAINT ON
THE OBLIVION OF THE DEAD

Ladies and gentlemen
Whose mother is no more,
The old gravedigger
Scratches at your door.

Six feet down
Is a dead man's place;
He hardly ever
Shows his face.

You blow smoke into your beer,
You wind up your love affair,
Yonder crows chanticleer,
Poor dead beyond the pale!

His finger at his temple,
Look at Grandpa half asleep,
Sister busy with her knitting,
Mother turning up the lamp.

One who is dead
Is quite discreet,
He goes to bed
Right in the street.

The meal was good, was it?
Now how is everything?
The little stillborn
Get almost no fondling.

On one side of your ledger
Enter the cost of the dance;
On the other, the undertaker's fee
To make your books balance.

      Life's a ditty
      With a hey-nonny-no.
      Eh what, my pretty,
         Do you find it so?

Ladies and gentlemen,
Whose sister is no more,
Open up for the gravedigger
Who raps at your door.

Show him no pity,
He will come all the same
To drag you out by the heels
When the moon is full.

      Importunate wind,
      Howl on.
      Where are the dead?
      They're gone.

CLAIR DE LUNE

It comes with the force of a body blow
That the Moon is a place one cannot go.

The world is yours when you advance,
Moon, through magical August silence!

When you toss, majestic mastless wreck
In seas where black cloud-breakers break!

Ah, if my desolate soul could mount
The steps to your pure baptismal fount!

O blinded planet, fatal light
For the migratory Icarian flight!

Great sterile Eye of Suicide,
The disgusted have convened, preside;

Icy skull, make mockery
Of bald, incurable bureaucracy;

O pill of absolute lethargy,
Be dissolved in our cranial cavity!

Diana with overly Doric chlamys,
Take up thy quiver, do thy damage.

With thy one dart inoculate
Wingless Love that sleepeth late!

Planet flooded with powerful spray
May one chaste antifebrile ray

Descend and bathe my sheet tonight
So I may wash my hands of life!

THE CLOWNS

Upon a white and starchèd ruff,
A neck that's equally as stiff,
Rests a hairless, cold-creamed face
Like hydrocephalic asparagus.

The eyes are drowned in the opium
Of universal self-indulgence;
The harlequin mouth casts a spell
Like a singular geranium.

A mouth which alternates the while
Between a glacial, uncorked O,
And the transcendental overflow
Of the proud Gioconda smile.

As they adjust the powdered cones
On their skullcaps of black silk,
The crow's-feet tighten round their eyes,
Their little noses pucker up.

In their rings the gentlemen wear,
For jewel, the Egyptian scarab;
The dandelion of vacant lots
Suits them well as boutonniere.

They feed on little but thin air,
On vegetables also at times,
Rice that is whiter than their costume,
Mandarins, and hard-boiled eggs.

As members of the Pallid Sect,
They have nothing to do with God; hence
Their motto: "All is for the best
In the best of all possible Mid-Lents."

II

Tattooed upon their pure white hearts
Are the maxims of the Moon.
"Brethren, let us think of death!"
Is their bacchantic watchword.

When a virgin passes on,
They attend her funeral,
With necks upheld as vertical
As candles carried to an altar.

A most fatiguing rôle to play
All the more so when no one
Waits at home to rub them down
With a conjugal ointment.

These lunar dandies feel, in fact,
That they are called upon to sing,
"If you please, my pretty thing,"
To each blonde and each brunette.

They are most certainly blasé;
And if you find them taken in
By the Skirt now and then,
That bit of efficacious gauze,

Rest assured they play the fool
To have below their learned heads,
As makeshift cushions on their beds,
The breasts of women they have loved.

See them stretching out their necks
Pretending they misunderstand
In voices delicate and bland,
And yet with such deceitful eyes!

All, moreover, most refined,
And in everything correct;
Theirs is the school of cromlechs,
And of factory smokestacks.

46

III

As they set out to molest
Statues in the parks at night,
Giving their arm and all that follows
Only to those the least undressed,

With woman in a tête-à-tête,
They act as if they were a third,
Call tomorrow yesterday,
And ask for Nothing, from the heart.

Confess their love but distantly
In an ecstatic toneless voice;
And follow up such silliness
With: "Ought we then, or oughtn't we?"

Till seized by some strange lunar need,
The lady swoons, and there you are:
Their arms have carried her quite far
From all convention has decreed.

IV

Overly rouged, in flowing sleeves,
On bended knee, they make their vows,
Much too vehement to be true;
Then whirl away in white jigs,

Bellowing: Angel, my meaning is clear!
This is a matter of life and death,
And then—but it's a waste of breath! . . .
They are willing, of course, to change their minds,

But ah, the fact that woman can
Still take herself so seriously
They cannot bear; they turn away
Roaring with laughter like madmen.

Be not too severe, oh, no,
You who are moved by a shapely leg,
Be not too severe, I beg,
On the white pariahs, the pure pierrots.

V

Little white choirboys of the Moon,
And eminent lunologists,
Their Church is open to one and all,
And brighter moreover than any known.

They tell us, with a gamy eye,
And very sacerdotal sleeves,
The scandalous world in which we live
Is one of a thousand casts of the die

In a game that one day Heart and Mind,
In order doubtlessly to see
Why they themselves had come to be,
Decided it was time to play.

And it is the best of all possible worlds,
And not a furnished room we rent
In lieu of one more permanent;
We are here, and made for one another.

They add, then, with a want of wit,
Since these gratuitous antinomies
Are after all not our affair,
The key to all is: So be it.

Brethren, the important thing
In life is to live but for the hour,
And though it call for all one's power,
To shrug one's shoulders at everything.

FOREWORD

My father, severe because he was shy,
Met his death with a solid jaw;
My mother I hardly ever saw:
At twenty life had passed me by.

And so before long I began to write,
But the Devil of Truth who hovered near
Would lean and whistle in my ear:
"Enough, poor fool, put out the light."

And being as hateful as they come,
I had no heart for marital bliss;
Women so readily say yes,
And stand entranced like the deaf and dumb.

You can understand why my life has been
A weathervane in the blowing breeze,
Changing its tune with perfect ease.
I speak for all you fine young men.

UNPARALLELED SEVERITY

There lay in an album,
Pale and wan
A dying geranium
Picked in Japan.

An exquisite ivory
Troubadour
Used harsh words
To the failing flower.

"A requiem, please,
For one so ill."
"I'm not in the mood,
Mademoiselle."

FIVE-MINUTE WATER COLOR

OPHELIA: Tis brief, my lord.
HAMLET: As woman's love.

Look, alas, the weather's turning;
Soon, ah, soon will come the rain.
People hurry here and there
To gather up the sheaves of grain.

> The boil bursts,
> The water falls;
> Oh, these wrangling
> Rain squalls.

Parasols
> Blossom out
All nature
> Is in rout.

On my sill
> A fuchsia,
> Looking like a pariah,
Revives.

SUNDAY PIECE

HAMLET: Have you a daughter?
POLONIUS: I have, my lord.
HAMLET: Let her not walk in the sun; conception is a blessing;
but not as your daughter may conceive.

Heaven, unmoved, weeps on forever,
Raindrops, shepherdess, dapple the river...

The river takes the Sunday air;
Not a barge is visible anywhere.

Vespers ring out overhead.
The shores are deserted, the lovers fled.

Girls file by in neat little rows,
Some already in winter clothes.

One, unarmed against the cold,
A sad gray figure to behold,

Leaves the others far behind,
And runs — Good Lord, has she lost her mind? —

And hurls herself from the lonely strand,
Unseen by boatman or Newfoundland.

Evening comes; the lights are lit
In the little port. (Ah, the old stage set!)

While rain continues to wet the river,
And Heaven, unmoved, weeps on forever.

GENTLEMAN

Declaiming

I have known them, known them all,
The matron and the pretty miss,
The easygoing, hard-to-get,
And what I've learned is simply this:
Flowers of flesh, however clad,
They vary with the time of day;
No word has power over them;
Men come and go, but women stay.
Nothing holds them nor makes them mad;
They'd have us all admire their looks,
Adopt the language of cliché,
And do what people do in books.
Without concern for vows and rings,
Let's drain the little they can give;
Their eyes are proud and monotonous,
Our respect is somewhat relative.
With little ado, let us pick what we can;
When roses wither, what can live?
And run all the gamuts possible:
I see no other alternative.

LADY

Declaiming in turn

If my appearance pleases you,
Do not stand on ceremony;
This is not a simple pose,
I am Woman, as you see.
Shall I wear my hair in braids?
I'm more enchanting with it down?
I know the art of every school,
My soul suits every man in town.
Gather the flowers of my smiles,
Feed on my lips and not my speech;
Anything more worth your while
Is far beyond all human reach.
We do not meet on equal terms,
You are only naïve men;
How can I extend my hand?
I, the Eternal Feminine?
My only object is the stars,
Fabulous Isis is my name;
If one could ever lift my veil,
Think what oases he would claim.
If my appearance pleases you,
Do not stand on ceremony;
This is not a simple pose,
I am Woman, as you see.

THE FLYING DUTCHMAN

Ugolino took his sons
Once upon a little ship,
With the pretext, the vampire,
Of giving them a free trip.

After five or six weeks,
When provisions ran low,
He said that he would not despair;
His boys were good, as boys go.

And then it came to drawing lots.
Such nicety! Such etiquette!
That man had a constitution
Almost nothing could upset.

And so, to keep the group intact,
The ancient stoic figure ate
His starving sons: the very fact
Is far too sad to contemplate.

Should this story bore you,
It is feeling that you lack.
Ah, but I am torn in two.
Mocking laughter answers back.

THE COMING OF WINTER

Sentimental blockade! Cargoes due from the East!...
Oh, rainfall! Oh, nightfall!
Oh, wind!
Halloween, Christmas, and New Year's,
Oh, my smokestacks lost in the drizzle, all
My factory smokestacks!

Where can one sit? The park benches are dripping and wet;
The season is over, I can tell you it's true;
The woods are so rusty, the benches so dripping and wet,
And the horns so insistent with their constant halloo!...

Ah, clouds pouring in from the Channel all day,
You have come to spoil our last Sunday!

The drizzle goes on;
In the sodden forest spider webs
Bend with the weight of raindrops and fall to ruin.
O Sun, potentate of the golden air
And the country fair,
Where are you buried?
Tonight a dying sun lies at the crest of the hill,
In the broom reposes on his side, his coat,
As white as the spit in some barroom,
He lies on a litter of yellow broom,
Yellow autumn broom.
And the horns call to him
To revive,
To come to!
Tallyho! Tallyho! Halloo! Halloo!
Oh, tragic anthem, when will you have done? —
And the horns sound cuckoo!...
And the sun, unattended, lies trembling off there
Like a gland ripped from the throat!...

57

Let us cry Halloo; let us cry Tallyho!
Good old winter is back, heigh-ho!
And, oh, the wide and winding road
With no trace of Little Red Riding Hood!...
Oh, those cart tracks left from a happier time —
In don-quixotic rails they climb
Toward cloud patrols the wind has rolled
Back to their transatlantic fold!...
Let us hurry, hurry, hurry — here's the season we know.
And the wind last night did a fine job, too,
Ripping up nests and lovely green gardens!
In my heart, in my sleep, I hear the blows of the axe!...

Green were the leaves on every bough,
But the thicket is a muck of dead leaves now;
O leaves and leaflets, may a good wind bear
You off in swarms to some muddy pond
Or may you find your way to some gamekeeper's fire
Or pad the mattress in an ambulance
For soldiers who are far from France.

Now is the time when rust invades the masses,
When rust gnaws into the kilometric spleen
Of telegraph wires on roads where no one passes.

THE MYSTERY OF THE THREE HORNS

A hunting horn upon the plain
Blares as long as breath holds out
To the quiet country roundabout.
From deep in the forest comes at last,
Loud and clear, an answering blast.
"Tantan!" sings one
To the woodland rills;
And the other: "Tantara!"
To the echoing hills.

The horn on the plain
Feels the veins
Swell in its head;
The other relies
On its lungs instead.

"Oh, where are you hiding,
Pretty horn?
How naughty you are!"

"I'm looking for my sweetheart
Who calls me from afar
To come and watch the Sun go down."

"I love you! Tallyho!
Halloo! Roncevaux!"

"Love is sweet, but don't forget
The lovely Sun is about to set!"

The sun divests himself of his pontifical stole,
And opens the gate of the sewer main
On rivers rich in golden gain
Which the most artistic
Of liquor dealers
Inflame with a hundred vials of oriental vitriol!...
The bloody pond spreads and spreads,
Drowning the mares of the Sun's chariot,
Which, rearing and splashing, settle
In these deluges of sulfur and alcohol!...

But the sands and cinders of the horizon
Quickly drink this display of poison.

Halloo! Halloo! Glory! Glory!...

And before very long the two have met
Face to face, disconsolate.

The wind comes up, the temperature falls;
Two have met: there are three in all.

Halloo! Halloo! Glory! Glory!

" — Let us go then, arm in arm,
But a drink for the road
Could do us
No harm."

They laugh in such a bitter way —
Pitiful horns! Pitiful horns! —
I hear them to this very day.

The hostess at the Sign of the Great St. Hubert,
When morning came, found them all three dead.

And they got the authorities out of bed
To ascertain what the cause might be
Of such an immoral mystery.

The horns, the horns, — the sad,
Sad horns!...
They go on and on now changing their tone,
Changing their tone and changing their tune,
Ton-ton, ton-ton, ton tone!...
Away on the north wind now is borne
The sound of the horns, the sad, sad horns.

But the echo remains; for I cannot change tone!...
This is the season; now vintage is done!...
Now come the rains so impossibly slow;
Good-bye wicker panniers, Watteau panniers, too,
That danced in the groves when harvest was through;
This is the time of the dormitory cough,
Herb tea drunk far from the family hearth,
The time when consumption will cast its pall,
And misery settle over all.

O flannels, hotwater bottles, pharmaceuticals, dreams,
Curtains parted on balconies along the strand
Before an ocean of suburban roofs,
O lamps and engravings, cakes and tea,
Have you alone remained faithful to me?...
(Oh, you and the sound of the lovely piano
And the sober, hebdomadal mystery
Of the vital statistics
Evening newspapers carry!)

This is the season, and the faltering planet!
Let the wild south wind
Unravel the slippers being knitted by Time.
This is the season — oh, heartbreak! — the season!
Every year without fail
I will try, as in chorus, to sound its note.

MOON SOLO

On the roof of a coach at night I lie,
My cigarette pointing to the sky;
While my poor bones jostle and roll, up dances my soul
Like some Ariel;
Without malice or solace, my lovely soul,
O roads, O hills, O mists, O vales,
My lovely soul — let's see what it entails.

Yes. We were madly in love, we two,
And with never a word drifted apart;
A sense of disgust held back my heart,
A disgust that was universal, too.

Her eyes said: "Now you see what I mean?
You mean to say that you haven't seen?"
Yet neither would be the first to act;
We longed to kneel *together*, in fact.
(Now you see what I mean?)

So where can she be?
Weeping her heart out bitterly?
So where can she be?
My darling, I beg of you, do take care!

O the woods by the road are cool and clear!
O shawl of sorrow, all things seem to hear,
And all willingly
Would trade places with me!
There is magic on the roof of the coach I ride.

By hoarding the coin of what must be,
Let us improve upon destiny!
More stars in the sky than pebbles by the sea
Where others than I have watched her bathe;
All goes under Death's dark wave.
No port but the grave.

Years will go by,
And each on his own will grow hardened somehow;
And often — I can already hear myself now —
Say to the other, "Had I but known!..."
But married, too, would each not on his own
Have also said, "Had I but known!..."
Ah, cursed from the start,
Dead end for the heart—
What an ass was I!

But wild for happiness then in truth,
What shall we do? I with my soul,
She with her fallible youth?
O my aging sinner,
How many evenings after dinner
Shall I turn to infamy to do you honor!

Her eyes would blink: "Now you see what I mean?
You mean to say that you haven't seen?"
But neither would be the first to act —
To kneel together. Ah, in fact!...

O see the moon climb,
Dream road beyond time!
We have passed the cottonmills, we have passed the sawmills,
And nothing remains but a few road signs.
And little pink cotton-candy clouds
With a thin crescent moon that continues to climb;
Dream road beyond sound, dream road beyond time...
What spacious, clean rooms
In these pinewoods where
Since the dawn of time
It is dark as the tomb!
Ah, for an evening of lovely abduction!
I people these rooms, in my mind I am there,
In my mind I behold a loving pair
Whose every gesture breaks the law.

And I pass them by, and I leave them there,
And lie back down
While the road winds on, Ariel, I;
No one waits for me, I am going nowhere:
I have only the friendship of hotel rooms.

O see the moon climb,
Dream road beyond time,
Dream road without end;
Now here at the bend
Is the posthouse where
The lanterns are lit,
And we drink fresh milk,
And change postillion,
While crickets trill
Under the stars of July.

O broad moonlight
Like a wedding of torches drowning my sorrow tonight,
The shadows of the poplars along the road...
The torrent that listens
As it flows...
A River of Lethe that overflows...

O Moon Solo, when
Will you answer my pen?
O this night on the road;
Stars — all there, all,
With all you forebode.
O fleeting hour,
Had I but the power
To retain your image until autumn returns!...

How cool it is now, how cool,
And what if now at this very hour
She also strolls at the edge of some wood
Drowning her sorrow
In a wedding of light! ...
(And how she loves to stroll at night!)
Having forgotten the scarf for her throat tonight,
She is sure to take cold in such cold, clear light!
Oh, my darling, I beg of you, do take care;
That cough is more than one can bear.

Ah, would I had sunk to my knees when I could!
Ah, would you had swooned in my arms as you should!
What a model husband in me you'd have found,
As the swish of your skirt is a model of sound.

PAUL-JEAN TOULET
(1867-1920)

CATHAY

You who have from far Cathay
　　By perilous convoy come,
While under the spell of opium
　　Or drunk with tea

In the palace of some paramour
　　When day dies in the west,
Did you then gaze upon Princess
　　Boudroulboudour

Whiter than luminous abalone
　　In her black pantaloon;
And then one night beneath the moon
　　Did John Chinee

Knock at your door, as bowed in grief
　　As the asphodel of Ouac,
And vow he'd sew up in a sack
　　His lovely wife

Who, though unfaithful, still was one
　　Who could from wind-swept rock
Rise, a shimmering white peacock,
　　In the rising sun?

FLIGHT

O great white-wingèd blackbird slowly, slowly veering —
A night of love between two Sundays disappearing.

BLACK GIRL

Yes, she is black. Her cheek has no rose tint,
No burst of gold like grain against the sky.
Coal, too, is black. But light a match to it,
And into flaming roses it leaps high.

PAUL VALÉRY
(1871-1945)

POMEGRANATES

Pomegranates, fruit whose hard
Rind to rioting seed must yield —
One would think that he beheld
The sundered forehead of a god!

If the heat that you have borne,
O pomegranates opened wide,
Has, with the irritant of pride,
Made you crack your ruby walls,

And if your desiccate, golden shell,
From pressure of some hidden force,
Breaks in brilliant gems of juice,

I, at this luminous rupture, turn
My dry thought inward and discern
The architecture of the soul.

HELEN

O Light, 'tis I, who from death's other shores
Have come to hear the cold wave climb the stone,
And see again a thousand ships at dawn
Emerge from dark to the beat of golden oars.

And now these lonely arms call back from night
The kings whose salty beards amused my hands.
I wept; they sang of dim and conquered lands,
And the gulf their beakèd vessels put to flight.

The echoing conch I hear and the trumpet call
Answer the rhythmic blade in its rise and fall,
The slaves' clear song that holds the sea in chains.

And watch the gods, exalted at the prow,
With a classic smile the bitter salt wave stains,
Extend their sculptured arms, forgiving all.

THE FRIENDLY WOOD

Pure were the thoughts that once were ours
When onward, hand in hand, we strode
In silence on the open road
Alone ... amid the sleeping flowers.

As if betrothed we wandered then
On where the verdant darkness led,
Sharing, like some enchanted bread,
The moon, belovèd of madmen.

And so we died; and far away
Alone upon the moss we lay
Deep in that secret, murmuring wood.

Above, in light that has no end,
Face to face in tears we stood,
My silent comrade, O my friend!

THE SYLPH

Unseen, unknown,
Essence am I,
Alive and dead,
On the wind blown!

Unseen, unknown,
Genius, chance?
I've but to advance
And the task is done!

Read, understood?
Ah, I delude
The minds of the best!

Unseen, unknown,
Between two robes,
A naked breast!

ASIDES

What do you do? Why, everything.
What are you worth? Worth, well,
The worth of mastery and disgust,
Presentiment and trial...
What are your worth? Worth, well...
What do you want? Nothing, all.

What do you know? Boredom.
What can you do? Dream.
And with the power of the mind
Can turn the morning into night.
What can you do? Dream,
And so drive boredom from the mind.

What do you want? My own good.
What must you do? Learn.
Learn and master and foresee,
All, of course, to no good.
What do you fear? The will.
Who are you? Nothing, nothing at all.

Where are you going? To death.
What will you do there? Die;
Nor ever return to this rotten game,
Forever and ever and ever the same.
Where are you going? To die.
What will you do there? Be dead.

MAX JACOB
(1876-1944)

LITTLE POEM

I remember the room I had as a child. The muslin of the curtains at the window was trimmed with scrawling patterns, in which I endeavored to locate the alphabet and when I made out the letters, I transformed them into imaginary pictures. H was a man sitting, B, the arch of a bridge over a river. There were several chests in the room with open flowers delicately carved on their wood. But what I liked best were two knobs on the pillars you could see through the curtains, knobs that I took to be the heads of puppets with which it was forbidden to play.

LÉON-PAUL FARGUE
(1876-1947)

MUDDY MADRIGAL

Dedicrudory stanza

Within my heart when you are here
Bunches of pickled herring bloom.
You go, I thrive; you reappear,
I sour quickly and leave the room.

VALERY LARBAUD
(1881-1957)

POEMS OF A MULTIMILLIONAIRE

(Poèmes par un riche amateur, 1908)

PROLOGUE

Borborygms! Borborygms!...
Rumblings of the stomach and the bowels,
Lamentations of the constantly changing flesh,
Voices, irrepressible whisperings of the organs,
Voices, the only human voice that does not lie,
And persists even for a while after physiological death...

Beloved, how often we have paused in our love-making
To listen to this song of ourselves;
How much it had to say
While we tried to keep from laughing!
It rose from the depths of our being,
Compelling and ridiculous,
Louder than all our vows of love,
More unexpected, more irremissible, more serious —
Oh, the inevitable song of the oesophagus!...
A stifled cluck, the noise of a carafe being emptied,
A sentence slowly, endlessly modulated;
And yet there it is — the incomprehensible thing
I can no longer deny;
And yet there it is — the last word I shall speak
When still warm, I am a poor corpse "being emptied"!
Borborygms! Borborygms!...
Do they also exit in the organs of thought,
Rumblings one cannot hear, through the thickness of the
cranium?

Here are, in any case, some poems in their image...

ODE

Lend me thy great noise, thy powerful, gentle gait,
Thy delicate nocturnal glide across illuminated Europe,
O luxurious train! And the agonizing music
Running the length of thy gilt, embossed corridors,
While behind the brass knobs of lacquered doors,
Millionaires slumber.
Humming I pace thy corridors
And follow thy course toward Vienna and Budapest,
Mingling my voice with thy hundred thousand voices,
O Harmonika-Zug!

I experienced for the first time all the joy of living
In a compartment of the Nord-Express, between Wirballen and Pskov.
We were gliding over fields where shepherds,
Under clumps of huge trees like hills,
Were clad in filthy, raw sheepskins...
(Eight o'clock one autumn morning, and the beautiful blue-eyed
Singer was singing in the neighboring compartment.)
Wide windows beyond which I have seen Siberia and the Mountains
              of Samnium,
Bleak, blossomless Castile, and the Sea of Marmara under a warm rain!

Lend me, O Orient Express, Sud-Brenner-Bahn, lend me
Your miraculous deep tones and
Your vibrant string-voices;
Lend me the light, easy respiration
Of your high, thin locomotives with their graceful
Movement, the express engines
Drawing effortlessly four yellow gold-lettered carriages
Throught he mountain solitudes of Serbia,
And farther on, through rose-heaped Bulgaria...

Ah, these sounds and this movement
Must enter into my poems and express
For me my inexpressible life,
The life of a child whose only desire
Is to hope eternally for airy, distant things.

THE MASK

Always when I write I wear a mask,
A long antique Venetian mask
With a low forehead
Like a great white satin snout.
I sit at the table and lift my head,
Gazing at myself in the glass, full-face
And then at an angle, beholding
The childish, bestial profile that I love.
Oh, if only a reader, the brother whom I address
Across this pallid, glittering mask,
Would come to plant a slow, heavy kiss
On this low forehead and wan cheek,
And bring to my face the full weight
Of that other, hollow and perfumed like mine!

L'ETERNA VOLUTTÀ

None of the sweetest things in this world:
Neither the perfume of faded flowers,
Nor music mid-ocean
Nor the faintness that comes
In a child's swing
When one's eyes are closed and one's legs taut,
Nor a warm, caressing hand on my hair
Filling my skull with a thousand little demons
Like musical thoughts;
Nor the cold caress of the organ
On one's back, in church;
Nor chocolate even,
Whether in melting cakes,
Cool at first, then burning to the tongue,
As fat as pigs,
As tender as the North!
Whether liquid and steaming
(Raise your heavy lips, colored girl,
So they may penetrate me until I am breathless,
Leaving a perfumed fire behind them
And a delicate moisture over my whole body! . . .)
Nor the almond flavor of certain rouges;
Nor the sight of things through red,
Mauve, or green windowpanes
As in the smoking-room of the Danieli in Venice;
Nor the precious feeling of fear,
Nor the perfume of lacquer, nor
The morning cries of roosters deep in the city; —
None of the most beautiful sights:
Neither the Mediterranean
With its own bitter, blue smell,
Its caressing, short
Rumple and beat
On the sides of ships.

(Oh, nights on the bridge — when not ill — with the watch-officer!
And you, Lookout, guardian angel of the crew,
How many nights I have spent, silent
At your feet, watching the stars in your eyes,
While Boreas whistled in our faces.)
The Mediterranean with its innumerable
Diverse islands,
Some white with the gray-green of olive trees,
Others golden with villages;
Others: long blue objects lying hidden,
Their straits laden with music,
Bonifacio, like the gates of death,
Messina with Faro, Scylla sparkling
In the night,
The Lipari Islands with their few lights (one high, red, and streaming);
And all day long
All this ocean
Like a great flowering garden . . .
No, none of these things,
None of these spectacles
Can ever distract me
From the eternal delight of sorrow!
In me you behold a man
Made completely mad
By the sense of social injustice
And poverty in the world!
Ah, I am in love with misfortune!
I should like to clasp it and identify myself with it;
I should like to bear it in my arms as a shepherd bears
The new-born lamb that is still sticky . . .
Give me the sight of all the world's sufferings,
Give me the spectacle of outraged beauty,
All shameful actions and vile thoughts
(I want to create still more sorrow;
I want to blow upon hatred as on a funeral pyre.)

I want to kiss contempt full on the lips;
Go tell Shame that I am dying of love for her;
I wish to sink into infamy
As into the gentlest of beds;
I want to do all that is justly forbidden;
I want to be saturated with derision and ridicule;
I want to be the most ignoble of men.
May vice belong to me,
May depravity be my domain!
I must avenge all those who suffer
(And neither can happiness itself be considered innocent);
I want to go farther than all others
In ignominy and reprobation,
I want to suffer with everyone,
More than everyone!
Don't close the door!
For I must go sell myself at any price;
I must prostitute myself, body and soul;
I am so hungry for contempt!
I am so thirsty for abjection!
And so many others have tasted them again and again; so many:
The Poor!
Alas, I am too rich, Misfortune
Is forever forbidden to me no matter what I do:
I am a Rich Man, naturally good and virtuous;
And if I were still richer, perhaps
I could afford Shame,
Sorrow, and the whole naked baseness of the world?
But let me hear at least,
Constantly rising toward me,
The cry of the World's sorrow.
May my heart be unspeakably filled with it;
And may I hear it still in my tomb,
And may the grin on my dead face
Tell of my joy in hearing it!

THE OLD STATION OF CAHORS

O traveler, cosmopolite! At present
Disaffected, put aside, retired from business.
A little back from the main road,
Old and pink amid the miracles of morning,
With your useless canopy
You extend toward the light of the hills your empty platform,
A platform once swept
By the airy, whirling skirts of great express trains.
Your quiet platform at the edge of a meadow,
With the doors of your waiting-rooms always closed,
And their shutters cracked by summer heat...
O station that has witnessed so many farewells,
So many departures and returns,
Station, double door open on the charming immensity
Of the Earth, which must somewhere contain the joy of God,
A thing dazzling and unexpected,
Henceforth you rest, tasting the seasons
Which return bearing the breeze or the sun, and your stones
Know the cold flash of lizards; and the wind,
Tickling with light fingers the grass about your rails,
Red and heavy with rust,
Is your only visitor.
The commotion of trains no longer caresses you:
They pass far from you without pausing on your grassy sward,
And leave you to your bucolic peace, station calm at last
At the cool heart of France.

ALMA PERDIDA

Vague aspirations; enthusiasms;
After-breakfast thoughts: flights of the heart;
Tenderness resulting from the satisfaction
Of one's natural needs; flashes of genius; action
Of one's digestive processes; calm
Of completed digestion; joys without cause;
Circulatory troubles; memories of passion;
Perfume of benjamin in the morning tub; dreams of love;
My enormous Castilian wit, my immense
Puritanical sadness, my special tastes;
Chocolate, candy so sugar-coated it burns, iced drinks;
Soporific cigars; and you, lulling cigarettes;
Joys of speed; delight of remaining seated; benevolence
Of sleep in total darkness;
Great poetry of banal things; diverse facts; voyages;
Gypsies; sleigh rides; rain at sea;
Madness of a restless night, alone with a few books;
Heights and depths of time and temperament;
Moments reappearing from another life; memories, prophecies;
O splendors of daily life and ordinary routine,
Yours, this lost soul.

POET'S WISH

When I have been dead for several years
And cabs in the fog still collide
As they do today (things not having changed)
May I be a cool hand upon some forehead!
On the forehead of someone humming in a carriage
Along Bromptom Road, Marylebone or Holborn,
Who, thinking of literature,
Looks out through the yellow fog at the great black monuments.
Yes, may I be the dark, gentle thought
One bears secretly in the noise of cities,
A moment's repose in the wind that drives us on,
Lost children in a vanity fair;
And may my humble beginning in eternity be honored
On All Saints' Day with a simple ornament, a little moss.

SCHEVENINGEN, OFF SEASON

In a bright little bar that was carefully waxed,
Cozy and warm behind the drawn blinds,
Over long English drinks we sat and relaxed
While a sea wind rattled the chairs outside.

A wardroom it was or a Pullman clubcar:
And I felt as tense as one does en route;
I was very much moved, I was gentle and far,
Like a well-mannered child with a lump in his throat.

But everything there was completely at ease!
At the bar they spoke so we couldn't hear.
How small one feels, how down on one's knees
On nights like this with the breakers near!

THALASSA

Seated on a couch at the rear of my cabin
And rocked like a doll in the arms of some mad girl
By the pitch and roll of the ship in rough weather,
I bear upon my soul this luminous circle — this porthole
Which might be a shopwindow where one offered up the sea;
And, in my somnolent state, dream
Of constructing, in a form as yet untried, a poem
To the glory of the sea.

O Homer! O Virgil!
O Corpus Poeticum Boreale! It is in your pages
That one must look for the eternal verities
Of the sea, for those myths expressing an aspect of time,
The fairylands of the ocean, the history of the waves,
Marine spring, and marine autumn,
And the lull preparing a flat, green path
For Neptune and his procession of Nereids.

I bear upon my soul this luminous circle as it travels
Up and down, now filled with the white-speckled, blue-gray
Mediterranean landscape, and a corner of pale
Sky, and now
The sky descends into the circle, and now
I sink into a glaucous, cold,
Whirling light, and now of a sudden
The porthole, blinded by foam, wheels dazzled into the clear sky.

On the constantly shifting line of the horizon,
No bigger than a child's toy, a white Roumanian steamer
Passes,
Meeting the waves as if they were deep ruts in a road, the screw
Emerging from the water and whipping up the foam;
And signals to us, dipping its ensign,
Blue — yellow — red.

Ship's noises: voices in passageways,
The creaking of the wood, the grating of the lamps,
The throbbing of the engines with their stale smell,
Cries swallowed by the wind, drowning the music
Of a mandolin which strums: *Sobre las olas del mar...*
The usual sound, the usual silence.

Oh, to think of the raging wind up there on deck, the pirate-wind
Which, as it whistles through the rigging, makes
Those stars and stripes of three colors
Crack like a whip!...

MY MUSE

Of Europe I sing, her railroads and theatres,
Her constellations of cities, and yet
I bring to my poems the spoils of a new world:
Shields of rawhide painted in garish colors,
Red-skinned girls, canoes of scented wood, parrots,
Arrows feathered with green, blue, and yellow,
Pure gold necklaces, strange fruits, carved bows,
And everything that followed Columbus in Barcelona.
You possess the force, my poems, oh, my golden poems,
And the surge of tropical flora and fauna,
All the majesty of my native mountains,
The horns of the bison, the wings of the condor!
The Muse who inspires me is a Creole lady,
Or rather the passionate slave the horseman carries
Attached to his saddle, slung across its crupper
Pell-mell with precious stuffs, gold vases, and carpets,
And you are conquered by your prey, O *llanero!*
My friends recognize in my poems
My voice with its familiar after-dinner intonations.
(All one has to know is where to put the stress.)
I am operated on by the invincible laws of rhythm,
I do not understand them myself: they are there.
O Diana, Apollo, supreme neurasthenic
Savage deities, is it you who dictate these strains,
Or is it but an illusion, something
Purely of myself — a borborygm, a rumbling in my bowels?

THE GIFT OF ONESELF

I offer myself to everyone as his reward;
I bestow the reward on you even before you have earned it.

There is something in me,
Deep within me, at the core of myself,
Something infinitely arid
Like the summit of the highest mountain;
Something comparable to the dead spot of the retina,
Which gives back no echo
But sees and hears;
A being with a life of its own, but one which
Lives all my life, and listens calmly
To all the gossip of my conscience.
A being made of nothingness, if such is possible,
Insensitive to my physical sufferings,
Which does not weep when I weep,
Which does not laugh when I laugh,
Which does not blush when I commit a shameful action,
Which does not complain when my heart is wounded;
Which stands motionless and gives no advice,
But seems forever to say:
"I am here, indifferent to everything."

It is void perhaps as is the void
And yet so vast that Good and Evil together
Cannot fill it.
Hatred dies in it of asphyxia,
And the greatest love never enters it.

Take all of me then: the sense of these poems,
Not what you read, but what comes through them in spite of me:
Take, take, and you have nothing.
And wherever I go, in the entire universe,
I shall always meet,
Outside myself and within myself,
This unfillable Void,
This unconquerable Nothing.

IMAGES

I

One day in a popular quarter of Kharkov,
(O that southern Russia where all the women
With white-shawled heads look so like Madonnas!)
I saw a young woman returning from the fountain,
Bearing, Russian-style, as Roman women did in the time of Ovid,
Two pails suspended from the ends of a wooden
Yoke balanced on neck and shoulders.
And I saw a child in rags approach and speak to her.
Then, bending her body lovingly to the right,
She moved so the pail of pure water touched the cobblestone
Level with the lips of the child who had kneeled to drink.

II

One morning, in Rotterdam, on Boompjes quai
(It was September 18, 1900, around eight o'clock),
I observed two young ladies on their way to work;
Opposite one of the great iron bridges, they said farewell,
Their paths diverging.
Tenderly they embraced; their trembling hands
Wanted, but did not want, to part; their mouths
Withdrew sadly and came together again soon again
While they gazed fixedly into each other's eyes...
They stood thus for a long moment side by side,
Straight and still amid the busy throng,
While the tugboats rumbled by on the river,
And the whistling trains maneuvered on the iron bridges.

III

Between Cordova and Seville
Is a little station where the South Express,
For no apparent reason, always stops.
In vain the traveler looks for a village
Beyond the station asleep under the eucalyptus:
He sees but the Andalusian countryside: green and golden.
But across the way, on the other side of the track,
Is a hut made of black boughs and clay,
From which, at the sound of the train, ragged children swarm forth.
The eldest sister, leading them, comes forward on the platform
And, smiling, without uttering a word,
Dances for pennies.
Her feet in the heavy dust look black;
Her dark, filthy face is devoid of beauty;
She dances, and through the large holes of her ash-gray skirt,
One can see the agitation of her thin, naked thighs,
And the roll of her little yellow belly;
At the sight of which a few gentlemen,
Amid an aroma of cigars, chuckle obscenely in the diningcar.

Post-Scriptum

O Lord, will it never be possible for me
To know that sweet woman, there in Southern Russia,
And those two friends in Rotterdam,
And the young Andalusian beggar
And join with them
In an indissoluble friendship?
(Alas, they will not read these poems,
They will know neither my name, nor the feeling in my heart;
And yet they exist; they live now)
Will it never be possible for me to experience the great joy
Of knowing them?
For some strange reason, Lord, I feel that with those four
I could conquer a whole world!

THE DEATH OF ATAHUALLPA

Pues el Atabalipa lloraba y dezia que no le matasen...
Oviedo.

O how often I have thought of those tears,
Those tears of the supreme Inca whose empire remained so long
Unknown, on the high plateaus, at the far edge
Of the Pacific — the tears, poor tears,
In those great red eyes beseeching Pizarro and Almagro.
I thought of them while still a child when,
In a dark gallery in Lima, I would stop
To gaze at this historic, official, terrifying picture.
At first one sees — a fine study in expression and in the nude —
The wives of the American emperor, wild
With sorrow, asking that they be killed, and here,
Surrounded by crosses and lighted candles and priests
In their surplices, not far from Friar Vicente de Valverde,
Lies Atahuallpa, on the horrible, inexplicable
Apparatus of the garrote, with his brown nude
Torso, and his thin face seen in profile,
While at his side the Conquistadors,
Fervent and fierce, kneel in prayer.
This belongs to the strange crimes of History.
Encompassed by the majesty of the Law and the splendor of the Church,
So extraordinary in their agonizing horror,
That one cannot believe they do not live on
Somewhere, beyond the visible world, eternally;
And in this very picture perhaps there will always
Dwell the same sorrow, the same prayers, the same tears,
Like the mysterious workings of the Lord.
And I readily imagine at this moment
As I sit here writing, abandoned by gods and men,
In my furnished suite at the Sonora Palace Hotel
(In the Californian Quarter of Cannes)
Yes, I imagine that somewhere in this hotel,
In a room dazzlingly bright with electricty,
This same terrible scene,

A scene out of Peruvian history
That is dinned into us as children there in our schools,
Is enacted precisely
As it was four hundred years ago in Caxamarca.

— Ah, let's hope that no one opens the wrong door!

EUROPE

"The sweetness of Europe."
Etienne Pasquier

To M. Tournier de Zamble
on sending him the manuscript of EUROPE

I here append a poem, Monsieur
Xavier-Maxence, for womankind;
One of the many, it is clear,
Which bear the imprint of a mind
As varied as the atmosphere.

To Pompier I own my style:
How well that classic author wrote!
He was so fluent, so facile:
His lesson I have learned by rote,
He's well worth anybody's while.

O my editor, edit for me
This final effort of my Muse,
The last, alas, in verity;
The Swan her larynx will abuse,
And the pool of inspiration dry.

Pleasure, whom I served as liege,
Doth now this noble mind defile;
To Broad and Floozy I lay siege
More than any Grecian isle,
And more obliging than *Oblige!*

I

Midnight at sea like so many other midnights at sea:
The Cunard liner softly aglide on the moonless ocean.
It would be warm, were it not for this wind.
The sound of the nearest wave: a splash;
And of the other wave a little farther off: a sprinkle;
And then the other: a distant roar;
And another, turning back, whispers: *Shh!*
And all the waves go on murmuring together.
The lounges below deck are filled with light,
And filled with ladies in evening gowns and gentlemen in black.
Taste, weak heart, the anguish of this hour.
Think of nothing but your childhood. What, you are weeping?
No, no, do not weep: listen to the gypsies
Playing in the restaurant aft...
Up forward, the poet stands beside his love
Who is reclining on a divan under her furs;
An angel she is, a Señorita, who, recalling
His presence from time to time, says in a low voice:
Mein Liebling!
And again the indifferent sound of the waves.
Look, a flash of lightning!
But no; that is not possible; the night is clear...
And still the wind and the endless sound of the waves...

Another! Out there, look!
Always in that same corner of the sky.
It passes like a scythe over a field of grain.
And then another;
It lasts but a second. One would think
It was a wheel turning.
There: it is passing...
I have watched the fire turn; the lighthouse like a madman,
A giant dervish, turning its flaming head in the night,
And with its vertigo of light
Illuminating the country road, the flowering hedgerow, the
                    thatched roof,
Illuminating the tardy cyclist, and the doctor's carriage on the moor,
And the deserted depths over which the liner moves.

I have watched the fire turn, and am quiet.
Tomorrow morning, passengers in the lounge, coming up on deck
Where the wind will sting their cheeks and their cold eyes,
Will cry: "Land!"
And grow ecstatic under their mufflers.

Europe, it is you, I overtake you at night.
I come upon you again in your sweet-smelling bed, O my love!
I have seen the first and farthest
Of all your millions of lights.
There, in that little corner of the earth, gnawed
By the Ocean which encircles immense islands
In the myriad folds of its unknown gulfs,
There lie the civilized nations
With their enormous capitals, so luminous at night
That even above their gardens the sky is pink.
The suburbs reach out toward the thorny meadows,
Lamps light the roads beyond the gates;
The illuminated trains cut through the divided hills;
The diningcars are filled,
The carriages, in black lines, wait
For the people leaving the theatres, whose façades
Rise glittering under the electric light
Whistling in milky, incandescent globes.
Cities speckle the night like constellations:
There are some on mountain tops,
Others at the source of rivers, amid the plains,
And even in the very waters that reflect their crimson lights...

"Tomorrow, all the shops will be open, O my soul!..."

IV

In Colombo or Nagasaki I examine the Baedekers
Of Spain and Portugal or Austria-Hungary;
And contemplate the maps of certain middle-sized cities,
And meditate on their succinct descriptions.
The streets where I have lived are all marked out,
The hotels where I dined, and the little theatres.
These are cities never visited by tourists
Where things are as unchanging
As words on a printed page.

One leaves the *pueblo* one fine morning to go
To the Estacion del Norte in the Fonda de Aragon
Antiquated bus. Be still,
Little city, I know you are faithful, I shall return:
To me Japan or the Indies are not far;
And next year, or perhaps in a few months,
From Barcelona to Seville, I shall take —
I'll have the courage to take! — the lumbering *Correo,*
And the Fonda de Aragon bus will again contain this traveler
And toss him about to the rattle of its windows
Through the narrow streets between the stage-set houses
Just as if he had left the night before and were returning
After a visit to the next town.

And you, ports of Istria and Croatia,
And green, gray and pure white Dalmatian coast!
Pola on a clear bay filled with warships,
Between grassy green banks, ships gaily
Bedecked with red and white flags under a soft sky.
Cherso, Abbazia, Fiume, Veglia, new cities,
Or cities that seem new, without one's knowing
Why; Zara, Sebenico, Spalato and Ragusa
Tipped like a basket of flowers beside the waves;
And the Mouths of Cattaro, where there is no end
To following the sea amid mountains
Crenelated with inaccessible Venetian citadels.
O Cattaro, little box, little fortress one might give

A child at Christmas — complete down
To the green soldiers on guard at the gate;
Little building box, filled
With an inexplicable perfume of roses.

And, after these countries cut from sweet-smelling painted wood,
Enclosed in the cool shade of austere and abrupt black mountains,
You, arid, steep vertiginous road of Montenegro,
From which one looks down on ships and Austrian forts
So small they seem viewed through the wrong end of a field glass.
(O Road of Montenegro! And Montenegran horses, what frights
You have given me in that old blue landau!)
The red coach flies forward
In this country of gray stone, where a single tree
Is as welcome as a whole forest,
In that gray and black country where in valleys
Deep as wells, one sees
Unbelievably small green, blue, yellow and clear gray fields,
                        framed in stone,
Like patches of Harlequin's tights fallen from the air.
But Njegos is a village of red and white, clear and gay,
In a valley hardly dry from the waters of the flood,
Sad roads around Cetinje (with its Belvedere); and at times
In the clear gray aridity of these mineral depths
Reminding one of lunar landscapes,
Suddenly, as if the stones spoke, a harsh,
Melancholy and even music bursts forth, filling
The rock-encumbered sky with a mounting fanfare.
And when one's soul has grown uneasy and knows not how to answer
These well-modulated voices heard on every side
In the absolute solitude,
Finally, at a bend in the road, appear the first ranks of a blue
                        and garnet regiment.
Then near Ryeka, where one sees, as if in a new world, the lake
                        of Scutari,
Are melancholy open-air shops, hung with strong-smelling cloth
                        of Turkey red,
And black-tasseled white Albanians sweep wildly by,
With pistols in their belts...

And while the great ships of the Orient and Pacific
Sleep u;nder their necklaces of light
In the immense Far Eastern port, I see again
From the window of the diningroom of the Grand Hotel in Cetinje
The low houses painted in somber colors,
And the sadness of the Slav cities, sadder
By reason of their exile here.
The enormous watchdog of the Grand Hotel Vuletich — Turk, I think
                     was his name — I seem
To see him again lying in the sun, good coffee-colored beast;
Asleep in the calm of the hamlet-capital . . . .
And now perhaps he is dead, poor fat Turk . . .

X

And you, Italy, one day I knelt,
You remember, and piously kissed your warm earth;
Region of Heaven (are you not of sapphire, azure and silver?)
Heavenly region, enchained
Amid waves which, for the exile,
Constitute another Heaven,
Italy, enchained by the Nereids like Andromeda,
As you are again here in thought,
I kiss with a sacred horror your belly
And your lovely thighs fecundated by the gods . . .

XI

At the end of a little sloping street, I recognize
That sky and that sea and that smell,
And run to you, O shore.
My blessed Welschland, sunlit Roman world,
There you are, glorious dunghills, divine rags,
Nude children, red-faced patriarchs smoking pipes,
Crones with black hands, loud adolescent girls,
And you, O Sea!
Leave me alone, alone with the sea!
There is so much to tell one another, is there not?
The sea knows my travels, my adventures, my hopes;
And it is of them she speaks as she breaks
On the granite and cement cubes of the wharf;
It is my youth she declaims in her Italian.

One moment we sing and laugh together;
But before long she is telling of someone else.
Let us hurl sand and pebbles at this forgetful woman,
And be on our way!

PIERRE REVERDY
(1889-1960)

SALTIMBANQUES

In the midst of the crowd, together with a dancing child, is a weightlifter. His blue tattooed arms call the sky to witness their useless force.

The child whose tights are too large lightly dances, lighter than the balls on which he is poised. And when he holds out his purse, no one gives. No one gives for fear of providing too heavy a weight. He is so thin.

THE MIND EMERGES

What a quantity of books! A temple with thick walls built of books. I cannot say how nor where I entered, but once inside, I choked; the ceilings were gray with dust. Not a sound. All those great ideas no longer stirred; but slept, or were dead. How hot and dark it was in this sad palace!

With my nails I scratched the surface, and bit by bit, made a hole in the right wall. A window it was and the blinding sun could not prevent me from gazing out.

There was the street but the palace was no more. I could already see other dust and other walls rising from the walk.

LOUIS ARAGON
(1897-1982)

ELSA'S EYES

Your eyes are so deep that leaning down to drink
To them I saw all mirrored suns repair
All desperate souls hurled deathward from their brink
Your eyes are so deep my memory is lost there

In the shadow of birds now the ocean roars
Then suddenly the day clears and your eyes change
Summer carves the cloud on the angels' pinafore
The sky's never blue as it is above grain

In vain the winds pursue the azure's griefs
When they sparkle with tears your limpid eyes make
Envious the heavens less bright after showers
Glass is never so blue as it is when it breaks

Mother of seven sorrows O watery light
Seven blades have pierced the color prism
Light is the more poignant which pricks between tears
The iris bored black is bluer by its grief

Your eyes in misfortune form a double breach
Where the miracle of the Kings is again revealed
When with beating hearts they all three saw
Mary's mantle caught in the crib of the child

A mouth may well suffice in the merry May
Of words for all the songs and for all the sighs
There's too little firmament for all the stars
With their secret Twins they had need of your eyes

The child who holds pictures before him for hours
Will strain his eyes less immoderately
When you stare from yours I know not if you lie
One would think the rain were opening wild flowers

Do they hide lightning in that lavender where
Insects give deliverance to their lusts
I am caught in the net of the falling stars
Like a sailor near death at sea in August

This radium from pitchblende I have obtained
My fingers I have burned on this forbidden fire
O paradise regained relost and regained
My Peru My Golconda My Indies your eyes

One beautiful evening the universe broke
On the reefs where the signal fires did arise
I looked and saw glittering above the sea
Elsa's eyes Elsa's eyes Elsa's eyes

C

I have crossed the bridges of Cé*
It is there that everything began

A poem from out a time long past
Tells of a knight who injured lay

Of a rose upon the pavement cast
Of a bodice with an open stay

Of a mad duke's castle the poem tells
And of the swans in the castle moats

Of the meadow where dances every day
An everlasting fiancée

A song I have drunk like icy milk
Of glories long and falsely spun

The River Loire takes my thoughts away
With all the equipment overturned

And the guns untouched with safeties on
And the tears which run the tears which run

O France O my forsaken France
I have crossed the bridges of Cé.

---

* Les Ponts-de-Cé, the four "Caesar Bridges" near Angers, have been the scene of repeated conflicts from the Roman period on. It was to this point in 51 B.C. that the Gallic hero Damnacus withdrew in disastrous defeat before the Roman legions, much like the French in 1940 before the German invaders. — *Tr.*

JACQUES PRÉVERT
(1900-1977)

IMMENSE AND RED

Immense and red
Above the Grand Palais appears
The sun in winter
And then disappears
My heart like that sun will also disappear
Like it my blood will all drain away
Will go in search of you
Beauty
My love
And find you one day
There where you stay.

RAYMOND RADIGUET
(1903-1923)

THE LANGUAGE OF FLOWERS
OR STARS

I lived for some time in a house where there were twelve young girls who resembled the months of the year. I could dance with them, but that was my only privilege; I was even forbidden to speak. One rainy day, to avenge myself, I offered each one flowers I had brought back from my walk. Some of them comprehended. After their death, I disguised myself as a bandit to frighten the others. They purposely took no notice. In summer we all went out walking, and each of us counted the stars. When I found one too many, I said nothing.

Can it be that the rainy days have passed, and the sky is closed again? Your ear is not quick enough to catch the sound.

TO A NUDE WALKING

Model yourself upon the hill
That is pregnant with the grape.
She might also be content
To wear nothing but vine leaves.

And yet with grassy shawl
And fur piece of the thicket,
With headdress and muff of thyme
Where hidden rabbits frolic,

She costumes her beauty
— And you, extravagant coquette,
Clothed only in your flesh,
April, you think it's summer!

105

PHILIPPE THOBY-MARCELIN
(1904-1975)

A LITTLE STREAM

This is not the broad royal path
Of great impetuous rivers.
It is a little stream
In the shade of the hills.

The animals know it
For its unlimited freshness
And the modesty
Of its meanderings.

It does not eat the land away
Nor move its bed.
Before reaching the sea
It is lost in sand.

It is only at night
When in secret it sparkles,
When the moon consents,
No one knows of it but me.

It is a little stream
In the shade of the hills.
And I bathed there at evening
When I was sad and desperate.

SONG

Living or dead, the one I love,
Who is she, does she also love me —
I would not know.
She is an unfortunate one.

She is tall and black,
Having vowed to dress in white;
And her soul, with vows also to the somber delights
Of melancholy.

She loves cemeteries,
And the evening breeze, which censes her,
Shakes as she passes
The poisonous urns of nightshade.

THE NIGHT OF MY RETURN

It was not yet dawn,
But I had risen,
Rubbing my eyes.
All about me slept.
The banana trees below my window
Shivered in the calm
Moonlight.
Then I took my head
In both hands
And thought of you.

PHILLIPPE THOBY-MARCELIN

YOU WERE HUMMING

You were humming a sad,
Obscene meringue,
While with wild excitement
I drummed on the iron bedstead.
A tree arched beside us,
Straining to hear.
We did not see it,
My love,
And yet how intrusive it was!

THE NOBLE SERVANT

Sarah they called you
And you came from Ja-mai-ca,
With that drawling English of the islands;
(But even better than your speech
Was your dish of rice and wild eggplant.)

Gigantic night whose lap we could reach
Only with the help of your hands,
It is thus we see you again,
That great violet laughter
Torn to the pulp,
Those tender polyp arms
Draining suffering and anger from us all.

Now being grown, we are surrounded,
Flesh and bone,
By devouring jackals,
— And you are among us no longer.

Having no offspring
This honorable poverty
We have invested for life
So that we may enjoy it to the full
When prisons crumble
Along with lies and the armies based on lies;
For in the end that will come,
And we shall have the patience to wait.

PHILLIPPE THOBY-MARCELIN

THE PATHETIC RUNAWAY

Was it by day or night
In joy or sorrow
Was it yesterday or forever
That he had reclined
On the lyrical grasses of the year

Drawing out his body
To the height of a spirit from Guinea
Drawing out his sex
In the slithering companionship of snakes
Springing forth
With the boldness of bamboo

Embracing
The immense
The secret
The terrible

And his ear bent to madness
(God having but His hand
On the wind's mouth)
He listened
Through the rhythmic pulse
Of his howling wounds
To the bloody beat of a dancing revolt.

RENÉ CHAR
(1907-   )

THE ASSEMBLED WHOLE

Sickle maintained in the disordered heavens
Even in the midst of morning and our frenzy.

Moon which goes beyond us to skirt the edges of the heart,
The heart remaining in darkness.
Bonds which nothing can break
Under the active heel, through chilling noons.

Already here, O vernal twilight!
We were awake, but have not stirred.

HERMETIC WORKMEN...

Hermetic workmen
At war with my silence,

Even the frost linked
To the windowpane offends you!
And the mouth, bold and dumb,
To which I bend!

I hear on every side prayers of forgiveness,
Then a roar, an unfurling,
Fugitives fleeing before the torch,
Tomorrow's sufferers in the thicket.

In the city housing it,
The crowd already grows impassioned.
The light which deceives it with lies
Is a drum in space.

Caught like wool on the thorns
Of the stream is my suffering.

111

RENÉ CHAR

TORN MOUNTAIN

Oh, the constant leveling solitude
Of tears as they climb the heights.

When the thaw declares itself
And an old powerless eagle
Feels his assurance return,
Happiness leaps forth in turn,
Overtaking them at the edge of the abyss.

Huntsman, my rival, you have learned nothing,
Who go slowly before me
Into death, which I contradict.

FESTIVAL OF THE HUNTER
AND THE TREES

Sung to the accompaniment of two guitars

Two guitar players, seated out-of-doors on iron garden chairs in a Mediterranean setting, spend a moment or two tuning up their instruments. Enter the hunger, clad in a canvas jacket and carrying a gun and a knapsack. Slowly and sadly he recites the first lines of the poem, accompanied softly by the guitars, and then goes off to hunt. Each guitarist in turn intones the section of the poem which falls to him, observing a silence after each quatrain, a silence swept by guitar strings. A shot is heard; the hunter reënters, and, as before, advances toward the audience. As the guitarists rise and come to stand on each side of him, he recites the penultimate section of the poem to the ever intensified sound of the instruments. Together the guitarists loudly intone the finale, while the hunter stands mute, with bowed head, between them. In the distance are burning trees.

The two guitars exalt in the person of the melancholy hunter, who kills birds "so the tree will remain," with the same smoking cartridge setting fire to the forest, one who acts out a contradiction consistent with the exigencies of creation.

THE HUNTER::

THE HUNTER:

Whether exploring the depths of the sky
Or perched with wings that are beating still,
Lovely birds, we only kill
You that no enduring tree will die.

The hunter departs.

FIRST GUITAR:

Is it toward freedom that you grope,
Toward the promise of an open wound
As you thrust upward from the ground,
Poplar with that ogival shape?

SECOND GUITAR:

The little child that you undress,
Briars that so slyly lace
The quarry, feels within his flesh
Your kiss and its transparent tongue.

FIRST GUITAR:

The dog that is hounded by the bell
Will whine, bark, and then give ground.
Dry magic slowly brings him round
Playing upon him with all its skill.

SECOND GUITAR:

Turtledove, my deep distress
Which slowly made your presence known,
At night you sing for me alone,
Your white wing beats on my fortress!

FIRST GUITAR:

Decoy ducks in the bitter cold
Call on the hunter's gun to leap
From out its cage so they may keep
Their fraudulent and muted hold.

SECOND GUITAR:

Together the oak and the mistletoe
Speak softly of their enemies,
The hard-boned woodsman who downs the trees,
The blade of the slender child, also.

FIRST GUITAR:

The panacea of raging fire,
Mantis, brings lightning from above
Into your night, where on thin shanks
You kneel before your violent loves.

SECOND GUITAR:

Sleep in the hollow of my hand,
Olive branch in thy new land.
The whole day will be lovely, too,
Even though morning was cut through.

*A shot is heard in the forest
and its echo reaches the guitars.*

FIRST GUITAR:

The lark when scarcely touched by light
Soars sparkling with the joy it sings,
And an earth of starved and hungry men
Gropes blindly toward this living thing.

SECOND GUITAR:

People walk forth, blaze a trail,
They carve out with a bitter knife
A staff that will support the life
And ease the weariness of men.

FIRST GUITAR:

Cypresses that hunters mark
With wounds on evenings cold and clear,
Between the sunlight and the sea
Fall your shadows warm and dark.

SECOND GUITAR:

If to dispute one cannot turn
Then must one exchange one's house
For that sheltering boulder whose
Horizon fades beneath a fern.

FIRST GUITAR:

Dear shade which we reverence so
In ancient minstrel calendar,
Arrange the grasses for the hands
And necks of lovers to undo.

SECOND GUITAR:

Heart gives its heart to some clear stream,
Hurls into it a smoking cartridge,
Feigning ignorance that the sea
Will bring the mystery back one day.

FIRST GUITAR:

Sorrow and time together straying,
What will brought the two together there?
Muted swallows, all surveying,
Keep careful watch over the pair.

SECOND GUITAR:

Cherish, when stones are put to flight
By the constant tramping of your feet,
Hunter, the little patch of light
That marks their place upon this earth.

The hunter returns.

THE HUNTER:

We must be seen walking indifferent in your midst,
Forest kept alive in the hearts of everyone,
Being far from all doors, almost wholly unknown.
Before the spark of the void,
You are never alone, who are wholly destroyed!

Light of the burning forest.

THE GUITARS:

Thank you, and Death is surprised;
Thank you, Death will not insist;
Thank you, this is the end of day;
And thanks to that living soul who well
Keeps in check the funeral knell.

117

SPANISH

FEDERICO GARCÍA LORCA
(1899-1936)

NARCISSUS

Narcissus.
Your fragrance.
And the depth of the stream.

I would remain at your verge.
Flower of love.
Narcissus.

Over your white eyes flicker
shadows and sleeping fish.
Birds and butterflies
lacquer mine.

You so minute and I so tall.
Flower of love.
Narcissus.

How active the frogs are!
They will not leave alone
the glass which mirrors
your delirium and mine.

Narcissus.
My sorrow.
And my sorrow's self.

FEDERICO GARCÍA LORCA

SONG LONGS TO BE LIGHT

Song longs to be light:
In the darkness it glows,
a filament of phosphor and moonlight.
Light knows not what it longs for;
within confines of opal
meets itself,
and returns.

EVENING

Three tall poplars
and one star.

The silence gnawed
by frogs is like
a piece of muslin pricked
by green lights.

In a river
a dry tree
has flowered in concentric
circles

And above the waters I have dreamt
of the dark girl of Granada.

SONGS OF CHILDHOOD

CHINESE SONG

The young lady
with the fan
is crossing the bridge
over the cold stream.

The knights
in long black coats
gaze at the bridge
which has no railing.

The young lady
with the fan
and the veils
is seeking a husband.

The knights
are already married,
married to tall blondes
who speak white words.

The crickets sing
in the West.

(The young lady
moves off through the green.)

The crickets sing
under the flowers.

(The knights
ride off toward the North.)

LITTLE SONG OF SEVILLE

Dawn was breaking
in the orange grove.
Little golden bees
were searching for honey.

Where can the honey
be hidden?

In the blue flower,
Betty.
In the blue flower
of that rosemary.

(A tiny golden chair
for the Moor.)

A chair of tinsel
for his wife.)

Dawn was breaking
in the orange grove.

SNAIL

They have brought me a snail.

Inside it sings
a map-green ocean.
My heart
swells with water,
with small fish
of brown and silver.

They have brought me a snail.

A SONG SUNG

In cold gray
the Griffon bird
was clothed in gray.
And there from little Kikiriki
whiteness and shape
were taken away.

To enter cold gray
I painted myself gray.
And how I sparkled
in the cold gray!

LANDSCAPE

Evening by error
clothed itself in cold.

Behind the mirrors,
troubled, all the children
are making a yellow tree
break up into birds.

Evening is spread out
along the river.
And an apple-red blush
trembles on the little tiles of the roofs.

126

NICANOR PARRA
(1914-   )

THE TEACHERS

Our teachers drove us nuts
with their irrelevant questions:
how do you add compound numbers
are there or are there not spiders on the moon
how did the family of the czar die
can one sing with one's mouth shut
who painted the mustache on the Mona Lisa
what are the inhabitants of Jerusalem called
is there or is there not oxygen in the air
how many apostles did Christ have
what is the meaning of "consubstantial"
what were the words Christ spoke on the cross
who is the author of *Madame Bovary*
where did Cervantes write *Don Quixote*
how did David kill Goliath
the etymology of the word philosophy
what is the capital of Venezuela
when did the Spanish arrive in Chile?

No one can say that our teachers
were walking encyclopedias
quite the contrary
they were modest grade-school
or secondary-school teachers I've forgotten which —
equipped with canes and frock coats
since we were at the start of the century —
why did they go to such trouble
to trouble us like that
except for reasons they would never own up to:
an overpowering pedagogical mania
and the darkest, emptiest cruelty!

The dental structure of the tiger
the scientific name of the swallow
a solemn mass has how many parts
what is the formula for sulfur trioxide
how to add fractions of different denominators
the stomachs of ruminants
the family tree of Philip II
The Meistersingers of Nuremberg
the Gospel according to Saint Matthew
name five Finnish poets
the etymology of the word etymology.

The universal law of gravity
to what family does the cow belong
what are the wings of insects called
to what family does the duckbilled platypus belong
the least common multiple between two and three
does light have dark patches or not
the origin of the solar system
the respiratory system of amphibians
the organs exclusive to fishes
the periodic system of the elements
the author of *The Four Horsemen of the Apocalypse*
explain the phenomenon known as mi-rage
how long would it take a train to reach the moon
what is the French for blackboard
underline the words ending in consonants.

The real truth of the matter
is that we could have cared less
who would bother with such questions anyway
at the worst they scarcely made us tremble
only gave us headaches
we were men of action
in our eyes the world was reduced
to the size of a soccer ball
and to kick it was our passion
our adolescent reason for being
we had championship games lasting until nightfall
I can still see myself chasing

the invisible ball in the dark
one had to be an owl or a bat
not to run into the adobe walls
that was our world
our teachers' questions
went gloriously in one ear and out the other
like water off a duck's back
without disturbing the calm of the universe:

The component parts of a flower
to what family does the weasel belong
the method of preparing ozone
the political testament of Balmaceda
the ambush of Cancha Rayada
where did the liberating army enter
insects harmful to agriculture
how does the *Poem of the Cid* begin
draw a differential pulley
and determine its state of equilibrium.

My kind reader can understand
that they asked more than was fair,
more than was strictly necessary:
how to determine the altitude of a cloud
how to calculate the volume of a pyramid
show that the root of two is an irrational number
learn by heart the couplets of Jorge Manrique
stop all this nonsense
today we have a championship game
but still the written tests kept coming
followed by orals
(the cleverest among us got screwed on some)
with the same morbid regularity
with which the bandurria announces a stormy passage:

The electromagnetic theory of light
how does a troubadour differ from a minstrel
do we say "a number *is*" or "a number *are*"
what is an artesian well
classify the birds of Chile
the assassination of Manuel Rodriguez
the independence of French Guyana
Simón Bolívar hero or antihero
O'Higgins' abdication speech
you're failing faster than sand in an hourglass.

Our teachers were right:
of course of course
our brains came out through our noses
you should have seen our teeth chatter —
to what do we owe the colors of the rainbow
the hemispheres of Magdeburg
the scientific name of the swallow
the metamorphosis of the frog
what did Kant mean by his Categorical Imperative
how to convert Chilean pesos into pounds sterling
who introduced the hummingbird to Chile
why doesn't the Tower of Pisa fall over
why didn't the Hanging Gardens of Babylon come down
why doesn't the moon fall to earth
the departments of Ñuble province
how to trisect a right angle
what are regular polyhedrons and how many are there
this fellow hasn't the slightest idea of anything.

I'd rather have had the earth swallow me up
than answer those wild questions
especially after the moralizing lectures
to which we were subjected day after day:
Do you know how much each Chilean
citizen costs the state
from the moment he enters the first grade
to the moment he graduates from the university?
One million six-penny pesos!

One million six-penny pesos
and they kept on pointing their fingers at us:
how do you explain the hydrostatic paradox
how do ferns reproduce
list the volcanos of Chile
what is the longest river in the world
what is the most powerful battleship in the world
how do elephants reproduce
who invented the sewing machine
who invented the balloon
you're failing faster than sand in an hourglass
you'll have to go home
and bring your parents
to speak with the Principal of this Institution.

And in the meantime World War I
and in the meantime World War II
adolescence deep in the school yard
youth under the table
maturity never to be
old age
          with its insect wings.

PORTUGUESE

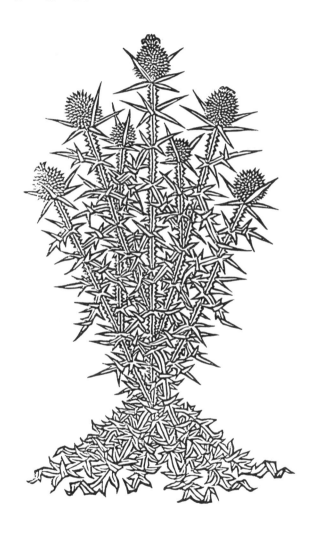

CASSIANO RICARDO
1895-   )

FIRST ULTRAVIOLET BALLAD

You do not for a moment imagine
that someone from a corner of the moon
is watching you right now
in your room.
You are naked — and all alone.
Untouched
by any gaze.
For you are sincere
only when you are naked and all alone.
You are being sincere
in so believing you are
where only you know you are —
in your intimacy.
In this strange moment
of absolute secrecy.

But mainly
because you do not even imagine
that someone — secretly —
between two hemispheres
is watching what you do.
Is following the little phases
of the metamorphosis
by which you are converted
from day woman
to night woman.
Until you become as naked
as a white object
before a mirror.

I am gazing now
on the two pink teats
from which the double bird
of the future sings.

JOÃO CABRAL DE MELO NETO
(1920-   )

THE ENGINEER

For Antônio B. Baltar

Light, sun, open air
envelop the engineer's dream.
The engineer dreams of clear things —
surfaces, tennis, a glass of water.

Pencil, square, paper,
design, plan, number:
the engineer projects an exact world,
a world no veil can hide.

(On certain afternoons we would go up
in the building: and the day-to-day city
like a newspaper read by everyone
gained a lung of concrete and glass.)

Water, wind, clarity —
the river on one side and the clouds above —
placed the building within nature,
growing out of its simple forces.

FERREIRA GULLAR
(1930-   )

THE PEARS

On the plate the pears
decay.
The clock above them
measures out
their death?
Let us stop the pendulum: Would
we thus postpone
the death of the fruit?
        Oh, the pears have tired
of their shape and
sweetness! The pears
have spent themselves
in the final glow of preparation
for oblivion.
                The clock
does not measure. It works
in a void: its voice glides
forth from the bodies of the fruit.

Everything tires
of itself. The pears are consumed
in their golden
repose. The flowers, in their everyday
flowerbed, burn,
burn in reds and blues. Everything
glides forth and yet remains intact.
                The common day,
everybody's day, is
the distance between things.
But the day of the cat, the feline
wordless day, that moves through the furniture
moves just to move on. Not through the furniture. But to
move on as I
move on: through the void.

The day of the pears
is its decay.

Is it tranquil
the day of the pears? They do not
cry like the cock.

                       Why
cry — when their song
is but an ephemeral
curve out of the heart?

Their singing must never
stop. Not because
their singing is the singing
men hear but
because, sing-
ing, the cock
knows no death.

THINGS OF THE EARTH

All the things I speak of lie in the city
    between heaven and earth.
All are things perishable
    and eternal like your laughter
    words of allegiance
    my open hand
or the forgotten smell of hair
    that returns
    and kindles a sudden flame
in the heart of May.

All the things I speak of are of the flesh
    like summer and salary.
Mortally inserted into time
dispersed like air
in the marketplace, in offices,
streets and hostelries.

    They are things, all of them,
    quotidian things, like mouths
    and hands, dreams, strikes,
    denunciations —
accidents of work or love. Things
    talked about in the newspapers
    at times so crude
    at times so dark
that even poetry illuminates them with difficulty.

    But in them I see you, new world,
    pulsating,
still sobbing, still hopeful.

AUGUST 1964

Past flowershops and shoestores, bars,
    markets, boutiques,
I ride
    in a Ferro-Leblon bus.
    I'm returning from work, late at night,
    tired of lies.

The bus jerks forward. Farewell, Rimbaud,
lilac clock, concretism,
neoconcretism, fictions of youth, farewell,
    for I must pay cash
    to buy life from the world's proprietors.
    Verse is suffocating under the weight of taxes,
and poetry is subjected to a secret-police inquiry.

    I say farewell to illusion
but not to the world, not to life,
my redoubt and my kingdom.
    From unjust wages,
    from unjust punishment,
    from humiliation, from torture,
    from terror,
we take something and from it construct an artifact

a poem
a banner

SUBVERSIVE

Poetry
when she comes
         respects nothing.
Neither father nor mother.
             When she struggles
up from one of her abysses
she ignores Society and the State
disdains Water Regulations
            hee-haws
like a young
   whore
   in front of the Palace of Dawn.*

And only later
does she consider: kisses
          the eyes of those who earn little
          gathers into her arms
          those who thirst for happiness
          and justice

And promises to set the country on fire.

---

*The presidential palace in Brasilia. — *Tr.*

141

MAN SEATED

Leaning back on this sofa
in the afternoon
in a corner of the solar system
in Buenos Aires
(intestines doubled up
inside my belly, legs
below my body)
                    through the living-room window
I see part of the city:
                    here I am
hardly supported by *myself*
by this thin body of mine, a mixture
of nerves and bones
living
a 98.6 degrees Fahrenheit
remembering green plants
that have died.

LINDOLF BELL
(1938-   )

POEM TO A YOUNG MAN

To Jorge Mautner

Let me play Love's last card
for the love of Death transfigures me.

Let me play Dark's final hand
for I need the deepest darkness to catch a flash of light.
Oh, how vast is my purity:
The world envelops me with its wings
and an angel with wings greater than its body
leaves the door open
and the fugitive
places the key under the rug
with a gold arrow indicating the spot.

Let me play the last card
for the night seems like a great fair.
A proud guest I go into solitude,
into the place of secret desire,
into the alabaster kingdom
and into the square with buildings
lacking the dimension of dark.

Weary of life,
let me play Love's last card,
for this is my niche, my body,
and my watchtower.

PORTRAIT OF AN
EX-YOUNG BOURGEOIS

They said to me: Smile
And I smiled with my teeth showing
as in an advertisement.
And I smiled with my mouth open onto space
onto the afternooons of life
onto the nights of life
onto the faces of life.
Smile, young man. Freedom
will open its wings
with their weights
and their pendulums.
Let the pliers extract the shout
and the revolt.
The sirens will place all things
in order.
And I smiled like a fish
with my pulverized mouth.
And I smiled! I smiled with the despair of the hour,
the hour of smiling.
And I smiled because of work
and because of life and death
and because of branches and foliage
and because of trees and rivers
and because of all the glories
and because of freedom the prostitute
and by smiling so much
I saw the vulgarity of the facile world.
HUMANITY HAS SCLEROSIS!
Smile, young man, smile,
for it is fitting for a young man to smile
and by smiling so much
I learned to confuse things and people
and to have a good memory of childhood
and of stupidity like a fruit I could not swallow.
Ah, offshoot of the gods, offshoot of man,

stone cherub in a stone square:
smile at anchorites and scapegoats
for the great joke continues.
All days are Ash Wednesdays.
Laughter remains in a straitjacket
and the smile is born of the abominable.
Smile. Let nausea ensue
for nausea is sweet.

And I smile. I smile at the siren songs of Society
and at the absinthe
and at the incense
and at the hailstones of ordinary happiness.
I smile at the crooked and immense
wail of life,
at rattles
and salamanders
and lustral waters
and kitchen utensils
and silver services
and I feel my body swell with an abcess.
And then I guffaw. I guffaw like a bird
or a wild beast, simple, impious, and without feeling.
AND I SHAKE ALL FOUNDATIONS.

ON HOPE

the poem
(that flower of struggle most perfect lotus)
grows
where in general nothing else will.
It needs neither money
nor honors.
It awaits neither promotion in official standing
nor a plaque unveiled to thunderous applause.

The poem grows
at the back of the house
where the louvered bathroom window opens.
Where the picket fence is falling to pieces,
rotting from neglect and poverty.
It grows in a place far removed
from general admiration,
far from literary movements
and passing fashions.

The poem grows
without fertilizers or manifestoes.
Complete in its own celebration.
Without the perfected techniques of plot construction
or the latest cibernetic findings.
Nor has it the least kinship
with framed diplomas
from Brazilian universities
or from foreign, interplanetary, or regional ones.

Since its destiny is to grow
it grows from the daily ashes
and from the filth of humanity.
It is the cud chewed in stables
and living rooms.
It spits furtively
on the head of pompous behavior.
The poem rises above
the wealth denied it
for lack of cunning and deception
in dealing with alien souls.
And green is its season
where it will forever
be futile to protect itself.

The poem grows from certain miracles:
from meal to meal.
From reconciliation to reconciliation.
From love lost to love found.
From God closing all doors
but leaving a crack
open for man's hope.
And from words, all these words
and their metamorphoses
that cross at the back of the house and of the world
and all the circumstances
by which I am crossed.

LINDOLF BELL

OF THIS CORE I SAMPLE
THE BITTER TASTE

Of this core I sample the bitter taste.
The taste of old fruit exposed.
                         To yearning.

Of this bitterness I sample
the bitter taste of slowly becoming
no more than a discernment,
a lucid epitaph, a part of oblivion.

Who knows if this bitterness is blood.
Who knows if this taste comes from water.
Or from vinegar or from grief.
Or if this bitterness is the earth.
Who knows knows everything
for everything tastes of bitterness.

No matter.
I sample this bitterness
like a face
that gazes at itself with fascination
and also with disgust.

I sample the bitter taste of this face.
And I love what I sample
                    for its bitter taste.

ON TIME

I'll be brief.
But not so brief
that eternity
escape the heart.

Because over the land
a dream
bit by bit
grows to its full.
It's my dream: of a just land
perfect
and shared by all.

It grows
while I wait and grow,
and I grow
little by little
to an entire time, an interior time
in the land of the pomegranate and the just dream
perfect
and shared by all.

I'll be brief.
But not so brief
that eternity
escape the heart.

ACKNOWLEDGEMENTS

Certain of these translations have appeared in the following publications; the translator thanks the editors and publishers for permission to reprint:

Poetry, vol. LXVII, No. 1 (October 1945).
Aragon: Poet of the French Resistance, edited by Hannah Josephson and Malcolm Cowley, New York: 1945. (Duell, Sloan & Pearce, Inc.)
Wake 12, 1953.
The Selected Poems of Federico García Lorca, edited by Francisco García Lorca and Donald M. Allen, New York: 1955. (New Directions)
Selected Writings of Jules Laforgue, edited and translated by William Jay Smith, New York: 1956. (Grove Press)
Hypnos Waking: Poems and Prose by René Char, selected and translated by Jackson Mathews with the collaboration of William Carlos Williams, Richard Wilbur, William Jay Smith, Barbara Howes, W. S. Merwin and James Wright, New York: 1956. (Random House)
Poems 1947-1957 by William Jay Smith, Boston: 1957. (Atlantic Monthly-Little, Brown)
An Anthology of French Poetry from Nerval to Valéry in English Translation with French Originals, edited by Angel Flores, New York: 1962. (Doubleday and Company)
Poems from France, selected by William Jay Smith, drawings by Roger Duvoisin, New York: 1967. (Thomas Y. Crowell)
The Streaks of the Tulip: Selected Criticism by William Jay Smith, New York: 1972. (Delacorte Press)
The Nation, October 8, 1973
Brazilian Poetry (1950-1980), edited, with an introduction by Emanuel University Press)
Antipoems: New and Selected by Nicanor Parra, New York: 1985. (New Directions)
Poems from Italy, edited by William Jay Smith and Dana Gioia, St. Paul, Minnesota: 1985. (New Rivers Press)

William Jay Smith, poet, critic, and translator, is the author of *The Traveler's Tree: New Selected Poems* and *Army Brat: A Memoir*, which tells about growing up as the son of an enlisted man in the Regular Army. Mr. Smith has written a number of books for children, including the popular *Laughing Time*. He compiled, with the late Louise Bogan, the celebrated anthology *The Golden Journey*. His poems have appeared in anthologies throughout the English-speaking world.

Jacques Hnizdovsky is a well-known painter and printmaker. He is an acknowledged master of the woodcut and has illustrated the poetry of Keats, Coleridge, and Hardy. His work hangs in the Boston Museum of Fine Arts, the Philadelphia Museum of Art, and The White House. Born in the Ukraine, he now lives in New York with his wife and daughter.